BELMONT PORTFOLIO

ALSO BY JOHN ROBERT LEE

St Lucian (1988)
Artefacts (2000)
Canticles (2007)
Elemental (2008)
Sighting (2013)
City Remembrances (2016)
Song and Symphony (2016)
Collected Poems 1975-2015 (2017)
Pierrot (2020)

ACKNOWLEDGEMENTS

Some of these poems have been published in *Acalabash.com, ArtsEtc,
Blue Mountain Review, filling Station*, *Illuminations*, *PN Review*, *Poems for
Ephesians*, *Prairie Schooner*, *PREE*, *Small Axe Salon*, *Sunday Jamaica
Gleaner*, *Temenos Academy Review*, *Voice of Saint Lucia*.

Thanks to:
Cover art: *"The Return" by Jackie Hinkson, Trinidad & Tobago, 2019.*
Author photo: Tara Lucien, 2022.
Jeremy Poynting, editor.
Hannah Bannister and Peepal Tree Press.
Artists, writers and musicians who inspired many of these poems.

For brief quotations from the work of W.H. Auden, The Bible,
Dionne Brand, C.P. Cavafy, John Donne, T.S. Eliot, Ilya Kaminsky,
Kes the Band, Li-Young Lee, Canisia Lubrin, Vladimir Lucien, Bob
Marley, Toni Morrison, Kathleen Raine, Roger Robinson, David
Rudder, Shadow (Winston Bailey), Philip Sherrard, Derek Walcott.

JOHN ROBERT LEE

BELMONT PORTFOLIO

P E E P A L   T R E E

First published in Great Britain in 2023
Peepal Tree Press Ltd
17 King's Avenue
Leeds LS6 1QS
UK

ISBN 13: 9781845235659

Supported using public funding by
ARTS COUNCIL
ENGLAND

CONTENTS

For
Veronica and Kamara

In Memoriam:
Alwin Bully 1948-2023
Gordon Rohlehr 1942-2023
George Lamming 1927-2022
Kamau Brathwaite 1930 – 2020
Michael Gilkes 1933 – 2020

"Ithaka gave you the marvellous journey.
Without her you would not have set out.
She has nothing left to give you now." – C.P. Cavafy

"We returned to our places, these Kingdoms,
But no longer at ease here, in the old dispensation,
With an alien people clutching their gods." – T. S. Eliot

"…but never guessed you'd come
to know there are homecomings without home." – Derek Walcott

"And when he came to himself…" – Luke 15:17

ARCHETYPES: ON STICKS OF OARS

(after Jallim Eudovic, sculptor)

The first men
who sighted those first cone peaks
rising from solfatara
imagined the firm breasts on their distant women
and loved her
loved this island place
place of flying-fish, herons and mountain fern
which they had reached
riding through salt air on their sticks of oars
bronze torsos set on tomorrow
bronze heads thanking the god of journeyings
bronze arms hungry to stop on starfish beaches
hungry for their women and children –
so they called her Iguana
after their first flesh-food, the green slow-eyed lizard
and they called her Home-of-my-heart,
they had seen her in lightning visions under mighty storms
riding through tossed air on their sticks of oars,
      her, open-mouthed like their women
      her, shy-beautied like their children,
riding through blue air on their sticks of oars
set from far, set on tomorrow, set for today –

the first men together, our first fathers
riding through evening air on long sticks of oars
harboured now in improbable dreams
harboured in fictions of remembering and Eudovic bronze
harboured in our distracted love
harboured, together.

BELMONT PORTFOLIO

(for Earl Lovelace)

Prologue: Belmont window, Saturday

some girl you never spoke with
some girl who walked on the other side of your road
some girl you looked out for from your blue window
lived in a house like this
behind hedges of croton and hibiscus
behind a wall with a gate and a mail box on it
behind bay windows and a red verandah –
maybe she was as shy as you
maybe she watched you between her curtains
maybe she wrote your initials on page 67 of her green maths book –

when you met her in New York years later
with your schoolmate her husband
you could not get past island gossip
and the vacuous opinions
to ask about her house
and the sacred memories you had scrawled on its cream façade.

i.   *ites, gold, green*

who will come to the red gate with the red mail tinbox
its pillars topped with red pyramids
who will walk past the yellow hydrant
and stare through the closed gate
at the thick variety of garden
wrought-iron barricade round the verandah
who will see the green banana leaf
peering over the grey wall
for who might come through the red gate on Pelham Street?

ii.   *somewhere in Belmont, yesterday*

maybe epiphany, maybe:
not what was, or will be, but what is
right there in your eye
angel wings, diaphanous, earth-corrugated
some annunciation, some mas revelation,
Rudder-Minshall creation incarnating
high art across the galvanise,
to raise up some good-looking seraphim
from the corner of Belmont Circular
to cross the Savannah
in the ricochet and dingolay
to ascend for a moment on Grand Stage
from troubled, narrow lanes of the fallen.

they don't believe anymore
they have abandoned joy in the dancing line
the amazing image, teasing metaphor
workshop camaraderie, shavings off the chisel
jam sessions in a small bandroom
smell of wet canvas
actors and dancers all over each other –

gone busy in the world, trying to catch their big names
no change to spare, time somehow impossible
become strangers to kindness, generosity, thankfulness
foreigners to their first neighbourhoods
the city's first pleasant suburbs
blue street-signs, winding alleys
intricate fretwork designs over open verandahs
tin mail-boxes on gates or walls
prayer flags in the gardens
multicoloured galvanise barricades –

now the houses age like lonely parents
rusting roofs, broken jalousies
walls crack like a earthquake pass,
next to younger nondescript blocks of concrete apartments
groceries, restaurants, fortified with burglar bars
and their forbidding character,
but it's the same everywhere in these islands
pushed down with debt, despair and indifference
divided among parties of pride –

do streets, suburbs, cities lose their joy
like artistes fixed on billboards
like critical hens of writers
like vain coteries of painters,
do they forget the first loves

strolling from the first red gates near the yellow hydrants
the first pan-runs somewhere on Jerningham Street
young Shadow and Rudder with their first lyrics down a Belmont lane,
forgotten the innocent vows in the old stone church
the first drums of the first Africans in Freetown?
I suppose –

but walking with my visitor's apprehensions
past this worn house, its satellite dish, its cracked wall
I raise my eyes to the spire-tip of Margaret of Antioch, Anglican
and from a room in the house
listen, a girl with a nice voice
singing with Kes the Band,

> *"if you comin' down from the mountain/*
> *Oh God oh/*
> *When de riddim beat is in town/*
> *See me jumpin' on de Savannah grass/*
> *de Savannah grass."*

and the joy that is
the sacramental grace that always is
lifts the house of I
to embrace with surging heart
Belmont Circular vernacular.

iv.   think of the Mystery

dear Belmont, given my intractable infatuations
my, I suppose, naïve expectations
and embarrassing enthusiasms

I meet Mystery incarnations
everywhere: brown heron on the Lea
fragrant marjoram in my front yard

intent gaze of a child across traffic
and here, on a Belmont gate,
teasing metaphysical speculations

the ubiquitous red mail tinbox
numbered 12A, Piscean number of completion,
with Alpha of the universe energies,

denoting harmony and perfection –
here, through the rusting gate
past the leaning, browning galvanise

under closed jalousies of the house next door
down the rough concrete walk
to what yard, what house, which Angel

of mercy, grace, unfathomable love
in what incarnation, in what masquerade
robed in what joy –

see, Belmont, my intractable infatuations
irrepressible imagination
my foolish certainty?

"*not another world, but this world experienced after another manner.*"
(Kathleen Raine).

on the third Day of the Creation Festival
the Ancients sit together
Earth in its mineral curve and design, Fadda
elegant water-bearing Plant in its clay pot, Mudda
young one clinging near with its tendrils, Alovera
and they chanted rumours in the Garden
of other Days to be imagined
to be imaged by Unimaginable
impossible cloud gossips of more coming
more than Earth-stone and Earth-plant?
noise of – galaxies? flying fish? sea birds?
and did you hear the Tree proclaiming like some Angel
"beasts, beasts" – what on earth are they?
beasts born of Fadda Earth? feeding on Mudda Plant?
and this Nancitori, this Nightmare:
Unimaginable will imagine in His Image
some Earth-Plant He calling A-dam!

in the neat stone garden of Villa Shalom
corner Pelham Street and Reid Lane, Belmont
in a back room somewhere
the cello player rehearses for a Festival play
called Silent Scars.

"if your clothes tear up/and your shoes mash up/you could still dingolay."
"I came down to the city/like a walking symphony." – Shadow

weeks toppling over Thursdays
so fast, is like the days shorten
and will soon be time to go, to leave
to kiss the last kiss, squeeze the last squeeze
prance the last dingolay
return like a stranger to the promise land –
in this October, your birth and death month
I YouTube your classic gothic, Dr. Shadow,
Belmont boy, raise with peas in Tobago
griot wailing from the Savannah
wailing down tracks
of your desperate notes
elemental, existential
excavating despairing desires
"what's wrong with me?"
off hungering, keening scales
of the bass melody
you rode like a midnight robber
watching for something, something
in the naked eyes of revellers
in the stripped eyes of lovers
in the wine of singers, dancers and flag woman
in the fretwork of the tenor pan
in the tired eyes of the old Brigade
in the mirror, in the mirror
watching for something, something
for God, really,
how else you explain
that perpetual empty space
out of which you hopped
standing in the same place

pulling from your guts
the plaintive chords
of those lost to themselves
in the hell of poverty –

so we learn Dr. Bailey, gothic Shadow, how to put the story:
hear in your ear a prancing line
chant extension of syllables through waving melody
phrase in the cave of your palate surprising phrases
straight from the yard behind the galvanise
"you don't need a bull dozer to become a composer,"
ricochet and dingolay and wave it
down in the common life you come from
Belmont, Laventille, Charlotte Street, Tobago,
stand up jumping in the parade of stanzas
with your rough, beautiful, holy voice.

vii.   leaving

leaving a place of passing infatuations
marking in your diary
a cartographer's route of various sentimentalities
tentative journeys across newly familiar streets, like
Queen's Park East into Jerningham Ave
left into Archer St, right on to Erthig Rd
left again on to Pelham St, crossing Meyler to find the B&B
corner of Pelham and Reid Lane. Ok –
ok, the beautiful front door of coloured glass
ok, the light-brown curtain tied like a shirt around a waist
ok, the quiet stone garden
camaraderie around the kitchen table
the view from a blue window
yellow hydrant and red mail box,
ok the galvanise fences, the once fine houses
the surprising steeple of Margaret of Antioch, Anglican
and ok the crowds in the Grand Market and deafening noise,
art galleries, plays, readings, concerts. Ok.
leaving, letting go of ambiguous embraces,
picking up the suitcase of the little you have
pulling up pegs of the tent sojourner, again
to go back where you started,
after the "marvellous journey" to some Ithaka,
until the next departure, next terminal
until… .. ok, leave that there –
so you bury in the pilgrim ground
behind the beautiful door of rainbow glass
and its diaphanous curtain tie like a shirt around a hip,
in the quiet, stone garden of fragrant herbs,
impossible infatuations
vague nostalgias
plotlines of shifty memory,
and board the narrow tube of the airport bus.

Epilogue: airport bus, rain

"forgive us this day our daily weakness/as we seek to cast our mortal burdens on your city, Amen/O merciful Father/in this bacchanal season/where men lose their reason../and if you know what I mean../let Jah be praised."
— David Rudder

strange old rubble wall
coming through the wet window of the airport bus:
different-shaded, different-sized stones
from sidewalk up to some indeterminate,
abstract, unfinished, uneven top,
looks blackened, as though burned,
and then, more even clay bricks finish the wall
which holds rust and red metal doors —
the humans of Port of Spain
walking past it, traffic lights and pedestrian crossing,
might know who the strange wall is and its story,
is it historical artefact, crumbling edifice forgotten by the council
an unknown artisan's work…
but it raining, the bus moving slowly in traffic
we look at bridges, torrential canals, white mosques,
bars and billboards cruising under drizzle,
the young people singing Chronixx, and
a category 5 hurricane beating up the Atlantic.

THE RETURN

(after Jackie Hinkson)

"If I feel the night
move to disclosures or crescendos,
it's only because I'm famished
for meaning;" – Li-Young Lee

persistent lament of wood-doves
who, who has gone, gone forever?

orange wafer of sun settling to horizon's eclipse

evenings shuddering with unrequited affections –

I would love you with ardent hunger
beyond your name, your ancient eyes, sensual lips
tattoo on your left breast
the inexorable news of your dying –

in this hour
in which I love you
I am a poem without a theme
without a clear image of you
a line to follow
a procession of remembrances to metaphor
no half-rhyme rhythms to match ambiguity –

going past your old house near the Baptist chapel
and Chinese grocery,
the blue estate-wall on my left with its crimson border,
trees behind it raucous with afternoon parrots,
a cock under the avocado tree crowing for some epiphany,
wanting a Creole love song from Philip Martelly and Kassav
to make me recall your alarming hips,
incomprehensible smile, perfect mouth,

your various infidelities,
like the turning familiar corner into which I bend my eyes
alert for unwelcome surprises –

how can I love you without you?

these November days close with apocalyptic cloudbursts over
darkening horizons;

who, who has gone, gone forever
wood-doves lament persistently.

SPEEDING AWAY

"Definition of expanding universe: a relativistic concept of the material universe according to which all celestial bodies are becoming steadily farther apart with the result that those more remote recede from the earth at greater speeds."

those who know such things
say our spiral galaxy, planets and further quasars,
the space-time continuum on which they curve orbits
are expanding fast, away from themselves
into some blueblack vacuum of solitary, dark matter –

like those cosmological stars
seems we are speeding away from each other
little time for intimacy of love's spaces
distracted by widening ellipses of the settled familiar
falling off into dark holes of self-centred universes –

there is a Heaven in which we speed towards each other
through infinite expanses of Spirit
dancing to holy nebulae carrying our names,
to enter welcoming celestial bodies
and an everlasting, ever-extending consummation.

COLLAGE
(for Ann-Margaret Lim)

"To the saints who are in Ephesus.." (Ephesians 1:1)

Gospelling yellow-breasts among avocado blossoms,
butterflies cavorting round the Rose of Sharon
(a clean white flower in the morning
tinged at noon with pink changings,)
hummingbirds probing under grapefruit,
hens and chicks foraging brown fallen leaves,
children on this Sabbath chanting hymns from their verandah,
and palm tree like a winged angel under the blue, sparse-cloud sky –

who would think
that pestilence is ravaging our world?

No safe zone on continent or island,
regular routines locked-down,
family, friends, lovers masked, distanced,
networks obsessed with flattening curves, death statistics,
churches and mosques closed, except for fanatics,
beaches, bars, brothels shut, except for sceptics
or those who want normal here, now,
and there are us crowding long lines outside shops –

who wrote the script
who configured this incredible dystopia?

Skies are clearing over megalopolitans everywhere,
Himalayas in view after decades,
I hear canals in Venice and Amsterdam are clean these days;
in neighbourhoods under curfew,
wood-doves, various warblers clock quick-passing hours;
crickets, breezes soughing through leaves, are the night sounds,
no backfiring bikes or late night dj's. Judgement is dropping abroad

from our mouths, our hands —

what unbelievable drama is rolling out behind the scenes,
Who is moving, Ephesians, to centre-stage of this cosmic scenario?

CHRONOLOGIES
(for Michael Gilkes 1933-2020)

> *"They are the city of the missing.*
> *We, now, the city of the stayed."* – Roger Robinson

Was conversation ever about anything else?
i.e. the contagion that falls from our palms
and those bitter mouths, i.e. the microbe
that ravaged with genocide and invasion of unwalled avenues,
that multiplied in fake genetics of dehumanization,
that burned the lungs of Hiroshima and Chernobyl, i.e. the viral germ
that made extinct, from pole to pole, fins, fowls, forests
of the Amazon and the steppes and the archipelagos and the first frontiers –

did we rage about anything else before we gazed regretfully
at empty boulevards behind our masked, averted eyes?

> *"I would like to find lodging the world depends on,*
> *some craft of soil and seashells unafraid of robotic*
> *futures…"* – Canisia Lubrin

We tried for a prophetic edgy abstraction of the new realisms,
spectral activists migrating through cafés of the embankment,
the sea wall, workshopped cities of our enchantments and seductions,
small-island Friday-night fish-fries, chapbook launches in art galleries,
party flirtations with full-bodied placard composers –

ephemeral as intense one-actor dramas,
that faith went somewhere with tired agnosticisms,
neglect and plain indifference, people fed up
with priests, stentorian prognosticators
and unbelievable theologies of change.

> *"Let us wash our faces in the wind and forget the strict shapes of affection."* –
> Ilya Kaminsky

A pornographic commodity purchased online with credit card debt
(never mind Disney's white fairytale endings,) soap-opera duplicities,
hardcore, incomprehensible dancehall lyrics and titillations,

and the more private exhaustions, frustrations, distractions
of infidelities, hungering for attention, affirmation, affection,
voluptuous faces and bodies strangers to the holy consummation

of their sexuality, their sacramental vocation – OK, I digress,
imagining busy sidewalks of sleeping beauties
who don't know their own loveliness and grace –

So what about love? Tell me.

> "…of course we'll exist, I
> suppose, but how, what would the world be with us fully in
> it, what about the 900 petroglyphs of our embraces." – Dionne Brand

At ziggurats, pyramids, gothic temples, peristyles, mosques,
their shamans interpret pundit chatter of networks,
conspiracy theorists and astrologers, as well as pizza nightmares,
via iPhone conference calls with lockdowns everywhere

because of the pestilence; Revelation, Nostradamus and dystopian fiction
feed anxiety and cabin fevers as do pharaoh, the czar and the president –

the eyes across the room, glances at bus-stops, that frank distanced stare
in a bank queue, mask lowered for an instant,

probing for *Imago Dei* in the mirror of your face, looking His likeness and image
in your cheekbones, your dimples, the returning love at your lips' edge.

> "There is only the fight to recover what has been lost
> And found and lost again and again: and now, under conditions
> That seem unpropitious." – T.S.Eliot

IKONS

"To the intent that now unto the principalities and powers in heavenly places might be known by the church the manifold wisdom of God." – Ephesians 3:10

What am I? Who is my name? What do I say now?
How to translate graffiti of hieroglyphs & petroglyphs
across catacomb stones, offer exegesis of heart prophesayings
sketched in blood-red above my head?
The plague slithers like mould across slave-built walls,
down lime-lined interstices to find goblet or platter
or complicit embrace.
What lonely disciple figured his fantasies in the sacred fish,
the holy X, the mark against the pestilential beast?

What now about now? What time is it? Where am I?
Days collapse across sundials with paranoid frenzy,
Sabbaths gather without us in their distanced pews;
crowded streets protest the mad president, monuments to hate,
tear-gas & batons in our faces, knees in our necks.
The pestilence is global, as are violence & corruption,
perennial trafficking in bodies & souls, the arrogance of blasted blasphemies.
Loneliness deepens, love & faithfulness are speculative fiction
imagined like some Disney fairy-tale
from pallets of the locked cells we are.
In these last days of exile, departure at hand,
I man hold the Lion of Judah high up
in all itations.
Whose earth is it? Why don't we see? Which word to listen?
What to talk now?
Who conceived grills in thick walls behind green windows
to hold black men who wore the *Imago Dei* across flaring noses & sensuous lips?
Who plotted their abduction & degradation from the Eastern land?
Who assaulted their wives & mothers beyond terrible imagination,
who gave themselves to such evil & why? why? Is any theory enough?
Is the answer hidden in metaphysics of antiquity, some Cain & Abel story?

Of course black lives matter, of course,
against barracoons of Gorée, coffles, slave caravels,
plantations, lynchmob klan, cops with their knees in our necks
cages of overcrowded prisons, doors of no return –
& we raise word against black-on-black hatreds,
corrupt black politicos, traffickers in black bodies today
& all continuing crimes on black creation.
Whose human it is? Whose earth it is? Whose judgement-word it is?
Soon come dread. Soon come. Jah.

How to hold love? Whose love is love?
What is love so insistent, so urgent, so hungering?
Why is love?
The isolation existential, confinement solitary.
Behind the 19th century brick fortress, through the narrow red window,
someone strains to look someone crossing the yard below.
Divine Mystery will not be contained against barred flesh.
Soul wants soul to union, beyond any possible translation
or theological exposition. That is Man.
We return from, we return to, each other & God.

& after, where? Who there? What to see?
After that thick, high door open for the last parole?
However you pass through.
Zion for the righteous sufferer,
Lion, Lamb, Dove on throne of ivory,
saints in gardens of herbs by the river of life
in light of rainbows high & lifted up,
like now, on the grey walls of Babylon.

ARIELLE (1966-2020)

"who tip toed into her own beauty like flowers" (Vladimir Lucien)

arrange your griefs
with white roses
wreaths & yellow lilies –

> her grace, elusive
> penetrating gaze, untranslatable
> smile at her lips' corners –

the purple balloon rises
above scraping trowels, hymns
appealing for remembrance, an unplanned tear
running off the cheek of a drizzling sky.

OFFICE HOURS

(for Charles Cadet, cantor 1924-2021)

Antiphon: "Nevertheless I am continually with Thee: Thou hast holden me by my right hand." — Psalm 73:23.

6 a.m.   Prime

First Monday morning of the year, cool
wind breathing hard through the java plum, avocado blossoms,
mango groves & hilltop antennas,
hens cuckling under the window, voices
of walkers in the road crossing dreams,
crickets in the bush, birds in the ficus hedges,
congregations of roosters calling to each other,
light on flowered curtains, beginning... .
Shuffling on waking knees we head to ablutions
& the first psalms of relief that we breathe
in another early hour.

The diary guides: renewal of covenant through today's devotion,
hopeful resolutions to close off last months' chores,
abandon lost causes, call estranged children
& open new files for new work that promises something more
than we've had before... well maybe... we pray...

9 a.m.   Terce

As you go out, take your mask, remember
to make a holy habit of distance
between sanitized palms & asymptomatic dimpled cheeks;
counter tops of tables, supermarket shelves, escalator railings
with memorized beads of public-service mantras;
plague has turned after us
with the calendar pages of this apocalyptic decade
like some medieval demon taunting exorcists;
town seems reduced, more empty lots, shuttered stores,
tattooed Babylon more pagan with blasphemies & obscenities,
sidewalk chorus a litany of infidelities, neighbourhood hatreds, politriks, decease
of popular citizens, over minivans' soundtrack of hardcore dancehall chant;

if your soul longs for the sacred scissor-tailed seagull, salt air, life,
come out to the beach-side food-vendor, get some peas dal
& sitting in the pew of your old car, offer grateful grace, so we pray.

12.00   Sext

& when, at the middle hour,
forgetful in pleasant flirtations of lunch-room banter
or snoozing off before the open document,
contemplating leaving the office early –
we had forgotten the ominous flags of the Reich on the autocrat's rostrum,
we had mocked conspiracy theories of ghosts in voting machines
& extraterrestrial paedophiles sighted in palaces & silicon-valley mansions –

when we had not taken the buffoon's narcissisms, lies, lawlessness seriously
& network news comes suddenly of insurgents in the rotunda of the Capitol,
broadcasts images of massed barbarian banners, battering rams,
insurrection of broken glass, military types scaling historic architecture,
plus tweeted rumours of hostages zip-tied under nooses in courtyards,
of trojan horses in the highest ranks of the national guard –
& phone lines are jammed & internet is dropping
& anxiety attacks since we don't know where those we love are,
& traffic is foul-mouthed, back-roads blocked with fools –

when these sudden reckonings come, like all shaking alarums
of the fall of bastions, public or domestic, cities or marriages,
old friends, close family, beloved pop-stars –
may we, O LORD, enter quickly, quickly days of rogation,
lifting fasting prayers against the enemy of our souls,
that we may rise fast above these disasters,
hear us, O Christ, we pray.

3 p.m.   Nones

Antiphon: "*But God commendeth His love toward us, in that, while we were yet sinners, Christ died for us*" – Romans 5:8

At the ninth hour, day falling to the multi-hued canvas of sunsets
off edges of islands' horizons, epiphanies multiply
with an egret's low swing over browning banana fronds
prancing in the breeze like New Year masqueraders,
with processions of robed grackles along electric cables over the dirt track
between hedges, & add bats darting from under eaves –
at a ninth hour on a sixth day at the crest of a now-mythical hump of a hill
at the turn of eras, outside a city which still wedges itself into our quarrels,
at a moment distant but too near for modern comfort,
at that ninth hour, a Man planted the pole of Himself
over lengthening shadows of the crossroads of our self-centred narratives
with His scourged, spittle-flaked, naked Body,
& if you will take it, to speak plainly in a familiar trope,
He slung a stone into the forehead of our last enemy
& became our Champion, if you will take it, will take Him –

post-modern folks don't care for our meta-narrative, &
post-truth just launched a coup of mobs against the Capitol;
Rome, her self-serving senators & colonies, call upon their deities
of the Stock Exchange, military-industrial complex, space-force,
conspiracy theorists & supremacist fundamentalists,
to preserve the Republic & so on from barbarians & aspiring emperors.
In the retreats of catacombs
we commemorate the ninth hour, the vacant grave, the reconciling Man
& rising against apprehensions, so, in faith, we pray.

6 p.m.   Vespers

"...in this hour of civil twilight all must wear their own faces" — Auden

Who walks with us through the dark tunnel of the spent day
whose kind arm surrounds aches & pains of aging limbs
whose gentle words lay to rest nagging worries
about health, children, dwindling finances, dying,
who meets us at the hour of incense
in the risen light of early evening over Emmaus,
in our verandahs having tea & what's left of new-year fruitcake,
in late traffic jams, in a solitary jog along the beach,
in the group keeping vigil beside the hospital bed & its ventilator,
in dark-brown benches of the empty chapel?

Say Holy, say Sacred, as final orange light over the sea's edge
comes like revelation through ikons on stained-glass windows,
as whistling wings and moan of doves nesting under grapefruit leaves
raise our eyes, hearts & murmuring lips to the sliver moon & her companion star,
& say Sacramental, & so, under the first planets & benediction
of cool air, so, let us pray.

9 p.m.   Compline

"What if this present were the world's last night?
Mark in my heart, O soul, where thou dost dwell," – John Donne

& after all is said, done, hoped, confessed
in this first Monday that was ours,
surrender thoughts, anxieties, plans,
to chirping crickets, rain's rhythms on the roof,
on the concrete footpath, to rain drumming
broad-eared, heart-shaped tannia leaves,
to the guardian street-light reflected in the mirror,
to the lonely dog gnashing at ghosts of shadows,
to the passing car blasting Lucky Dube,
to your faith companion laughing in her sleep,
to the bathroom clock dropping hands inexorably off its dial;
surrender twinge of toothache, tossing leg,
your unmasked, restless, contrite heart –

surrender to rest,
since tomorrow belongs to Mystery
& you have in store mighty promises
of inheritance, of translation, of a never-ending Hour,
so we know, so we have prayed. Amen.

12.00   Lauds

"...for he looked for a city which has foundations." (Hebrews 11:10)

how can the last way out
not be a dirt-track
moving under a canopy of trees
their dark barks turning white,
green foliage bowing over your passing,
& somewhere in all that good bush
angels stroll, you are sure, fluting like ground-doves,
their wings breezing above like casuarinas
near the beach-stone edge of Pigeon Island —

you gave me this Bible-text card
with that dirt-track road
between green trees
& their whitening barks
when we met in the City of Palms
in that city of refuge, city of priests,
& beyond my chaste prayers
my chastening desire
you pressed my hand to your lips
& left it there
all these kind years —

I have kept it in my Book of Offices
all your faithful hours,
all this becoming, as they say, one flesh,
& it is, I think
a true sighting,
on that sacred card with its scripture text
of the last road I want to walk with you,
the road that goes, my love,
to the City of Holy,
angels fluting like wood-doves

down the last dirt-track of Earth
beside the grace-filled trees
& their whitening barks.

So, with love, we pray.

"... *without participation in God there can be no escaping fragmentation, disintegration, self-alienation...*" – Philip Sherrard.

Note:
After W.H. Auden, *Horae Canonicae* (1955) and Hilary Davies, *Exile and the Kingdom* (2016).

The Canonical Hours/Liturgical Hours/Divine Office are times within which the sacred offices of prayer and contemplation may be performed. 6 am to 6 pm follow the Jewish 12-hour day, so 9 am is the 3rd hour, noon is the 6th hour and 3 pm is the 9th hour. The Latin titles of the hours are given.

APRIL

(for Anthony 'Cocky' Baptiste Jn., drummer (1964–2021))

on this first afternoon of your last April
sadness plays the fool
as news of your death sounds
like knuckling of a kenté drum
through the sunlit April of your last afternoon –

(this April   masquerade prancers   moko jumbies
goatskin drummers   are not allowed   to dance
your last   parade)

UPRISING

"O earth, earth, earth,
Hear the word of the Lord." — Jeremiah 22:29

Like all our garbage throttling oceans, the barrage
of horrendous news from every corner of this fatigued planet
deadens us to suffering life in war zones, famine-plagued villages,

race-baiting sidewalks, grief-stricken ICU wards, streets of homeless children
& aging dementia, numerous catalogues of pain
to which we have grown numb, dumb & frankly, bored —

hearts & minds are choked with junk, vain
matter on which we feed neglected souls,
desacralized spirits, if you allow me to invoke *imago Dei,*

the sacred space made for holy, holy, holy — like deep-sea
coral, pearl-making oyster, supple divine dolphin,
fluting whales, all that depth-diving aquamarine multitude

that we throttle with careless plastic capital —
we need, we need to rise to life, rise to see our fall
from the grace we were gifted, rise with hearts leaping to do right,

rise like silver flying fish over clean waters of living oceans,
like scissor-tailed sea birds over life-giving heritage,
rise up over our ravaged, sorry earth.

WATCHMAN
(for George Goddard)

*"Son of man, I have made you a watchman for the house of Israel; therefore
hear a word from My mouth, and give them warning from Me:"*
— Ezekiel 3:17.

I.   Babylon — City of Man

Ask native peoples who trusted paper promises
ask Africans chained below decks of slave caravels
ask Asians & other immigrants from islands of the sea,

ask them about liberal democracy that plants burning crosses
on their lawns, knees in their necks, metal in their fleeing backs,
that makes them invisible ciphers fenced in minority ghettos,

that gives power to autocrats who suppress their votes,
ask. This is Babylon. This is its system of privilege.
This is Nimrod's land, Babel in the plain of Shinar.

But ask colonies of Babylon, provinces of her Empire,
kanaval & cricket places, multi-cultural, many-racial,
all kinds of religions & no religion, sun, sand, sex

for cruise ships, petty tyrants & their micro-corruptions,
their traffic in diamonds, ivory, children,
their golf courses, multistorey condos,

ask the colonised in their complacencies, comforts & shopping malls,
ask about the muted mutterings, even at their ease in Babylon.

II.   Chant down Babylon

The dread-locked prophet comes every day to his box under the flamboyant tree
in the square by government house, facing the cathedral,
with people passing through to taxi stand & restaurants,

& every day mockers give him talk when he chant down the system,
chant down Babylon, bloodfire scandals,
point with his shaking finger at the pride & selfishness

of the busy metropolis; & he chant down
meaningless religion, church & state complicity,
idols of liturgical masquerade, big pomposity,

what god they know? & he chant down
the unspeakable corruption that everybody know about,
that everybody doing, rich & poor, that he cannot even mention in public;

& prophet chant down the oppression of poor like him,
no job, food scarce, shack leaking in rain, boss man wicked, virus in the air,
sick can't buy medicine, children don't have computer, politician door close;

& he raise his mouth against party garrisons & their barons,
if you don't vote for them, krapo smoke your pipe, you suck salt,
even your family don't know you;

when he look, he see the good book true,
lust for dollar & cents is root of all evil, all crime in the city,
everybody have a price, everything have a cost,

when you poor you like dog! This Babylon! This slave colony of Babylon!
& he come out against racism in Amerikkka, classism in his own island,
against hatred for people who different —

& the prophet start to bawl when he see what they doing
with their garbage, to the fish with their plastic,
how they cut down trees to build hotel & warehouse

& more golf course. & prophet chant & he chant & he chant
all the way to his little place outside the town.

III.   Zion – City of God

Son of man, man born of woman,
Watchman lying on his back in the sea
gazing at sea birds

loving the green hills in the blue distance
admiring children laughing with parents on the sand
hearing a sweet reggae melody coming across the water;

he certain that a new world near,
that the Most High planning new heavens & new earth, Zion,
far from Babylon, where righteousness rule,

& the prophet give thanks, laugh loud,
is peaceful, as he listen to the Spirit moving in the casuarinas.

ENDINGS

"Time has no future" (Toni Morrison)

endings. not conclusions. yesterday's memoir. tomorrow's fantasy.
today's fraying edges of old lace.
democracy's partisan tyrannies. logic and reason: assassins hunted.
your tattooed body like a Basquiat graffito. going to fat. distanced and masked.
among supermarket shelves, news of another gone to Sheol.
alone with modest groceries. grown shy of eyes and chatty mouths.
so many fallen apart like decaying brown leaves under breadfruit trees
in the abandoned garden. past passions tune themselves on the car radio
with Marvin Gaye. how see each other again beyond duty and polite
inattention. how fill our lips and arms and legs with each other,
again. endings. memoirs. fantasies. waiting now
for the epiphany of our selves, beyond loneliness, beyond
desire for the passing, the trifling, already forgotten —
endings. not conclusions...

PART TWO

"...the end of all our exploring/Will be to arrive where we started/And know the place for the first time." — *Four Quartets*, T S Eliot.

1.   What remains to be said, written and sung?

What remains to be said, written and sung?
We have been to the end of history and back again.
We have returned from cities of perfection,
come again to narrow lanes of Belmont,
sat in the King's halls of Cambridge, re-entered Marchand,
walked with laureates in Boston, Stockholm, Castries,
climbed hills of shanties above Fort de France,
swam in Skeete's Bay, Barbados,
drank over late-night fish on Baxter's Road, Bridgetown,
laughed with reggae stars and kaiso kings,
strolled pagodas in Tokyo, temples in Kyoto,
and prayed in simple pews of village churches –

love has left wrinkled skins of loneliness,
children gone to far countries, as they must,
lovers distracted by diversions of age
and old flames rekindling dead wood –
what remains to be sung, made poetry of,
of all those gone so quickly hours?

All of it I guess, that voyage of a life,
if you are brave enough to find
metaphors of the metaphysical in it,
in all the messy stuff,
the sacred and sacramental
in certain failures,
in bird-call insisting, insisting,
pup saying something to a goat in the yard,
konpa music coming up the hill,
child shrieking somewhere in a house,
and so on, all of it *there*,
in your present timeline,
in your hearing, *now*,
now threading that life and its inebriated days,

your weary hunger for affection, for affirmation,
the shifty-eyed hope of faith, of redemption,
years inevitably winding in their spiral
to that moment of the epilogue of your biography.

So, write it down and say it like a kaiso griot,
like Stalin or Shadow,
sing it strong,
like a chantwel over shak-shak, drums and violon,
like Bob Marley still wailing from passing vans
over the lost cities of yards.

Over the lost cities of yards,
unchanged sprawl of townships,
hill-squatting favelas, impossible Asian slums,
inner cities invisible to their 5th and other avenues –

drones and multiple Orwellian eyes cruise
among gulls, hawks and vultures,
while skies over Sudan, Palestine, Ukraine and such places
shower meteors of fire and germs
upon children and the old
hiding under their denuded masonry of homes;

inflation, supply-chain shortages, fuel prices
enter our partisan quarrels, local gossip,
pandemic-shadowed lives,

and we try to *see* Irina, in Kyiv,
playing Chopin on her ash-covered piano
in the bombed-out debris of her house.
What do we *see*? What does it mean?
What epiphany under that apocalypse?
What imagination confronts unreasoning tyranny
with defiant chords?
What shekinah sets tongues of fire in the streets,
shatters glass underfoot?
And sent this Etude to us as certain accounting?

3.   *And sent this Etude to us as certain accounting.*

"The holy stones lie scattered/at the head of every street." – Lamentations 4:1

And sent this Etude to us as certain accounting
to apostate patriarchs, right-wing religious
and pew warmers who applaud invasion of coveted territories
and capitols, mass graves of disappeared patriots,
thefts of voting rights, knees of bigots in black men's necks,
children in cages at borders and all such discriminations
against the *imago Dei* in skins and bodies they despise –

what, what do they know of the transcendent, the immanent,
the Presence of the sacred ikon they carry in pharisaic processions
behind ancient gold crosses on which they crucify afresh
the hated, betrayed, raped, bombed, the massacred children,
the Lord Immanuel.
What, what do they know?

4.   What, what do they know?

"burnin' all illusions tonight" (Bob Marley)

What, what do they know
they and their cabals
of oligarchs, bankers, generals
crime bosses and petty clerks –
of petroglyphs of memorials in ancient texts
of fluted psalms in forgotten catacombs
of Sumerian tablets relating diluvian epics stored in lost grottoes
of trumpets roosting in apocalyptic pages –
of blues harmonicas in late-night clubs
of blind singers in halls of arrogant empires
and kwéyòl lamentations on aching violons
of reggae prophets in Trench Town gullies
folk chanters every time, everywhere,
chanting down Babylon
pushing back beasts of earth and sea
heart crying from roots of keyboards the certain accounting
beyond here, beyond now, from time, from far,
trodding to its Zion, from Inferno to Paradiso
through this Purgatorio?

Through this Purgatorio
we press on, island travellers,
companioned with faithful, patient guides,
poets, players of strings and horns, cantors of songs,
Bunny Wailer, Patrick St. Eloi, Walcott, Kamau,
Billie Holiday, Sesenne Descartes,
metaphysical masters, psalmists,
mighty prophets, the disciples of the Ascension
and all that went before
and all that is to come –

I have not forgotten the friends of those young years,
including Alwin, Milton, Lelia, David, Theodora
and Carlton, Ikael, Fish, Pat, Paba –
our music: Elton John, Carole King, Marley, Jimmy Cliff and reggae icons,
zouk and konpa, Kassav, Malavoi, Shleu-Shleu, Exile One, Tabou Combo,
the Saint Lucian dance bands and folk musicians with clay-rooted voices…
and theatre, the first poems, parties, loves, the yards and all else…
today they are imagined narratives of drifting thoughts with all those
gone hours… gone to their travels, you wonder if your remembrances
are the same… we return from, we return to…
become stranger to the once familiar…

But you have become a stranger too…
collared in faith in agnostic seasons,
cloistered in chapters of a meta-narrative largely discredited,
proclaiming apocalypse, not idealistic democratic or marxist future,
calling the unthinking church to search its secretive corners…

these days, death is the familiar masked interloper
separating faces in telebituaries
from all they once held dear: their barbecued pork,
their living rooms, beds, cars,
phones, their books, their pulpits,

islands and cities they loved in,
their prizes, their money in the bank,
favourite children, partners,
seeing, hearing, breathing...
and they die, and with its eulogies
faith must tread carefully...

6.   *Faith must tread carefully*

"faith is the substance of things hoped for, the evidence of things not seen."
— Hebrews 11:1

Faith must tread carefully,
sandalled with the truth you wear,
as sparing with praise as a Japanese woodblock print,
lacing the essentials with fine lines
of compassionate portraiture,
leaving spaces within the frames
for wreaths of cherry blossoms
or bougainvillea cascading —

in these seaside cemeteries of small towns,
we are not theocracies,
forgotten autocrats decay alongside revered democrats,
Rastas share the palimpsest of sand with Vatican,
Muslim with Hindu, gay with straight,
believers with unbelievers,
political flags rot entangled between graves,
only love will rise from the dead
into the Presence of the Almighty,
(how you translate this is your business) —

in the supermarket
I see a photograph of a man I vaguely knew
above a book for written condolences,
while hidden speakers pipe
popular music, the days' hits, afrobeat,
which young people passing between shelves
are singing: is it Bruno Mars, Sevana, Chronixx? —
(am dropping names of the few I know,
suspect I'm wrong,)
but standing in line to the checkout,
I would dance if I could, something creative,

something stretched, extended, like Rex Nettleford,
against all the entombing thoughts
ghosting up too often now,
haunting against my faith in the Tree of Life,
my certainty of the empty tomb,
my ancient, treasured map to the City of God,
my island-pilgrim's progress.

7.   *My island-pilgrim's progress*

"So what is the odyssey/who is the meaning of this journey-../this life that presses on/under bird song in the mangoes.../how do they translate?" – Lee

My island-pilgrim's progress,
Saint Lucian,
: through a Caribbean parish of blue-hued hills,
surf over veined ocean, beaches
that have always been there,
scissor-tailed sea-birds that translate
the metaphysics of my metaphors
into sacramental messengers
bringing exegesis of sacred texts,
gliding into poems that circle
the fauna and flora of this creation
and its parting veils of the promised new beginning –

: through the capital of Castries, kwéyòl villages down the coast,
the intriguing lives, their complexities, their fundamental mystery,
their drums and violons, shak-shak and mandolin,
chantwelles and dancers in *wòb dwiyèt,*
Wailers reggae and Shadow kaiso in the bars;
and yes, new generations of a digital age,
rough-edged, pants below hips,
tattoos across breasts,
music hard-core and dance-hall…
but it's complicated,
and judgement must be compassionate –

: through this island today, wracked by politics and religion,
theatre, bookshops, libraries, galleries in decline –
media with its wearying gossip of talk-shows,
incessant, incomprehensible noise;
add contentious democracies of internet,
feeding insatiable desires of sidewalks, marketplaces, watering-holes…

but then, approaching mid-seventies, what do I know?

Poet and preacher, is this an "enigma of arrival",
the predictable "Pilgrim's progress"
to the "Celestial City," to "Paradiso?"
The "Odyssey", and a return from... a return to... of "The Prodigal"?

Past inevitable fatigue,
(to speak plainly),
in poetry surfing brooding lines,
this island pilgrim
bears the Caribbean voice
to the table of world literature,
placing there in canticles,
our accents, our history, our songs, our dances,
that in particular celebrate our apprehensions
of the Sacred, the Divine, the Transcendent and Immanent,
Alpha and Omega, the Holy City,
Incarnate Christ, Pantocrator.

ABOUT THE AUTHOR

JOHN ROBERT LEE is a St. Lucian writer who has published several collections of poetry. His short stories, poems, essays and reviews can be found in many journals (print and online), newspapers and international anthologies.

Among Lee's latest publications are *Pierrot* (Peepal Tree Press, 2020), *St Lucian Writers and Writing: an author index of published works of poetry, prose and drama* (Papillote Press, 2019), *Collected Poems 1975-2015* (Peepal Tree Press, 2017), *elemental: new and selected poems* (Peepal Tree Press, 2008).

In 1993, at the launching of a poetry collection by Lee entitled *Translations*, Nobel laureate Derek Walcott said of his younger contemporary, "Robert Lee has been a scrupulous poet, that's the biggest virtue that he has, and it's not a common virtue in poets, to be scrupulous and modest in the best sense, not to over-extend the range of the truth of his emotions, not to go for the grandiose. He is a Christian poet obviously. You don't get in the poetry anything that is, in a sense, preachy or self-advertising in terms of its morality. He is a fine poet."

ALSO BY JOHN ROBERT LEE

Collected Poems 1975-2015
ISBN: 9781845233518; pp. 212; pub. 2017; £10.99

John Robert Lee's *Collected Poems* tell both of a continuing journey and a subtly changing voice but also of an underlying, consistent attempt to hold together in one space the things that matter. This is seeking first the kingdom of God; maintaining the community of men and women who incarnate that kingdom and make life meaningful; the beauties of St Lucia's natural world and its rich traditions of folk-culture; and the challenges and demands of poetry.

Whilst sometimes Lee's poems involve a quiet self-communing, more often they are conversations with God and with those people who are close to him. At points they rise to being canticles of praise that express the experience of, or the yearning for the transcendent through the imagery of the visible world. And whilst the poems connect to the wider world of travel and world affairs, their touchstone is always St Lucia. Like Derek Walcott, like Kendel Hippolyte, Jane King and now Vladimir Lucien, John Robert Lee's poems demonstrate how possible it is to find an enriching, puzzlingly complex and intellectually stimulating world in a small island society.

The journey the poems tell is from the young man enthused with the energy of the radical decolonizing spirit of the 1970s, the years of deepening of Christian faith to the present of maturity and the acceptance of loss as well as gain, and the stamina needed for the continuing struggle for St Lucia to emerge from its colonial past and be ever more itself. In the later poems there are more glimpses of the private man who recognises that "My heart holds rooms I've never entered/ doors concealed, secret entrances." And whilst over the forty years of the poems one hears always a personal, signal voice, over time the poems increasingly invest in the Kweyol language of the St Lucian folk as well as the voice of the English master and, latterly, display an growing interest in the relationship between poetry and the visual arts.

Pierrot
ISBN: 9781845234782; pp. 72; pub. 2020; £9.99

The sacred and the profane, dialogues with self and world, literature and politics meet in the figure of Pierrot. He is the sad clown, holy fool of literary tradition, the suffering artist who connects to Christ in his most human incarnation as Man of Sorrows, and he is also the Pierrot Grenade of Caribbean carnival, the most literary of carnival figures who can spell anything, who carries a whip, but lashes with his tongue. The two meet so that Pierrot is both the bedraggled figure at the sordid end of carnival who is weary of the "Infernal cycles of mamaguy kaiso politricks", and the risen Christ who, if you listen, you can hear "crack His midnight robber word".

In his ninth collection of poems, John Robert Lee contemplates his 70th year in St Lucia and the sad chimes of mortality as friends and literary and cultural heroes leave this life. It's a time for a weighing up of where domestic, political, literary and spiritual journeys have reached. It is a time of both honest admissions but also renewed faith in all these journeys.

If any of this suggests a retired poetry steeped in reflective sorrow, far from it. This is the most vigorous, demotic and experimental of John Robert Lee's collections. There are new explorations of poetic forms such as the glosa, homages to the poetry of writers from Dionne Brand to Francis Thompson, the literary equivalent of the ekphrastic poems that have been appearing in his recent work. *Pierrot* is probably the most intimate of Lee's collections, more of the man in all his guises appears here, a confessional voice lightened by self-irony and humour. Sometimes Pierrot is an archetypal figure, sometimes he may be thought to be Lee himself. And if salvation is the ultimate prize, few have beaten down the Babylon of the great northern neighbour with a heavier, more righteous lash than Lee wields in his poem, "Who made me a stranger in this world".

PRAISE FOR *BELMONT PORTFOLIO*

In *Belmont Portfolio*, John Robert Lee has managed to refine a poetic voice as unassuming and plain-speaking as the places he chronicles, a voice that knows that as much as the universe spirals away from us into impressive, widening gyres of increasing abstraction, taking with it the people and places we felt we knew, it also coils towards us, sometimes lovingly, sometimes in wrath, but ultimately always bringing redemption. Yet it is also about an in-built and triumphant resistance to total fragmentation which we see in the poet's frustrations, hurt, disappointment, joy, hope and celebration – all part of a yearning for connection which he shares with the universe herself. The poet, like the universe, assumes his poetic duty to keep things close even as they must (also) recede. This is the message that he, the chronicler of the infinite in small places and in honest, quotidian experience comes to bring us… no big "project" just: "maybe epiphany, maybe:/not what was or will be/ but what is/ right there in your eye."

– Vladimir Lucien, Saint Lucian poet, essayist, author of *Sounding Ground*, winner of the overall OCM Bocas Prize for Literature, 2015.

*

As in his previous *Pierrot*, Lee addresses a variety of themes and concerns like the inevitable passing of time, missed opportunities, chance encounters, and the constant presence of "Babylon" in the world. The Covid pandemic broke out just after the publication of *Pierrot*, and of course it looms large in this new work.

The title of this new book refers to a suburb of Port-of-Spain where the poet briefly stayed. Belmont is well-known as the birthplace of both Shadow (Winston Bailey) and David Rudder, two famous calypsonians. The poet visits or revisits this suburb and is at first dismayed by the decline of a traditional way of life and the Calypso tradition, but encounters a sudden epiphany when he hears a young girl singing a song by the Soca group Kes The Band. The epilogue to this long poem is quite wistful as the poet leaves Trinidad with young people singing Chronixx's songs and a hurricane "beating up the Atlantic".

A constant theme in this collection is the plight of "these islands pushed with debt, despair, and indifference, divided among parties of pride" where Babylon always raises its ugly head, where profit and corruption always seem to win. But the poet is not defeated and enters into a dialogue with Shadow and David Rudder.

Lee is also well aware of the Caribbean literary tradition and his poetry contains Walcottian echoes like the references to the scissor-tail birds and the "galvanise" of Caribbean roofs. A number of poems are dedicated to well-known Caribbean poets and critics like Michael Gilkes, the Saint Lucian poet George Goddard, and the Jamaican poet Ann-Margaret Lim.

The last untitled poem-cycle in *Belmont Portfolio*, which forms Part Two, is a real tour de force and manages to end these varied "metaphors of the metaphysical" on a hopeful, positive note. In spite of a certain weariness or "inevitable fatigue", the poet still succeeds in making a major contribution to Caribbean and world literature, and this is after all, his achievement.

— Eric Doumerc, Senior Lecturer, University of Toulouse-Jean Jaurès, Toulouse, France

*

Prayer-haunted sensual musings of the Mystery of the Sacred in the journey through the iconic, shape-shifting infatuating Belmont, Port of Spain, birthplace of ikons Rudder and Shadow. This island-pilgrim trods well-loved streets, fallen lanes, (pan)yards, lost cities and Savannahs; spies through windows, and is teased and taunted by Belmont Circular vernaculars, breasted mornes, King's Halls, laureate Boston, gullied Trench Town, Saints, follow him or not, but confront a dystopian pestilence that upends life, turning old cars into pews as the contemporary horror of Northern Babylonian blasphemies knee breath from black bodies and defiant Irinian chords defy bombs and fiery debris. But, all is not lost for, "Soon come dread. Soon come. Jah."

— Anna Kasafi Perkins, Catholic theologian, Jamaica.

This collection by John Robert Lee is bound to be treasured by poetry lovers because herein is what one may call 'God's plenty'. It is truly admirable that, located in the beautiful environs of Saint Lucia, the poet allows his passionate mind to travel extensively to explore and examine distant lands, civilizations, cultures, customs, society, polity, religious doubt and faith visible on planet Earth. Like an impressionist painter, John adroitly makes use of his love for variant colours to create pictures of paradoxical reality that deeply stir the mind and touch the heart.

– Nibir K. Ghosh, India-based writer, critic, academic and Chief Editor, *Re-Markings*

Belmont Portfolio may be John Robert Lee's best book so far. It begins with a wonderful meditation on a sculpture by Saint Lucian Jallim Eudovic, which the poem reads as an origin myth, the voyage of "the first men together, our first fathers" crossing the sea to St Lucia. Written in a troubled time, the poems don't hesitate to go where the trouble is, "chanting down" corporate despoilers of the planet, hatemongering authoritarian politicians, and our culture's habitual deformation of the *Imago Dei* that resides in every human being.

Yet *Belmont Portfolio* is no grim Jeremiad – quite the contrary. It celebrates "the joy that is / the sacramental grace that always is" with praise-songs to calypsonians, painters, sculptors, dancers, and writers whose art radiates that joy – as do these poems themselves.

– Paul Breslin, Professor of English, Emeritus, Northwestern University, Evanston, IL USA.